D0866315

Why the Sea is Salty

A tale from Korea

Retold by Rosie Dickins
Illustrated by Sara Rojo

Reading Consultant: Alison Kelly
Roehampton University

Long ago, the sea wasn't salty like it is today. Once, it tasted sweet.

So where did the salt come from? Well, it all began with a magic millstone...

This millstone belonged to a great King.

Most millstones are used for making flour. But this millstone was different.

It made gold and jewels...

or special spices...

or whatever the King asked for.

The King's treasure chests were always full. His food was always delicious. And it was all thanks to his magic millstone.

One day, a thief heard about the millstone. “I want it!” he thought.

"How can I find out where it's kept?" The thief scratched his head.

Then he put on his best clothes and went to the palace.

The thief told the guards he had come from far, far away, just to see the palace.

A kind guard showed the thief around. "These are the gardens," said the guard.

"This is the throne room,"
said the guard.

"And that is the royal bedroom."

"I'm sorry not to see the magic millstone," said the thief. "I suppose it's hidden?"

"Of course," said the guard, with a laugh. "It's the King's greatest treasure."

"I bet I can guess where it is," said the thief. "Up a chimney?"

"No," said the guard.

"Under the floor?"

"No," said the guard.

"I bet you don't even know where it is," teased the thief.

"Yes, I do," said the guard proudly. "It's under the King's bed!"

"What a clever hiding place," said the thief.

"And I suppose you have to be a great magician to work the millstone?"

"Oh no," said the guard. "I've seen the King. You just have to tap it like this..."

"...and tell it what you want."

The thief left the palace, smiling.

Later, when no one was looking, he crept back again.

He tiptoed into the King's bedroom and reached under the bed...

The thief hid the millstone under his cloak. And he ran away as fast as he could.

He ran all the way to the sea. There, he leaped into a boat and sailed away.

Out at sea, he looked at the millstone. "What shall I ask for first?" he wondered.

"Maybe some food would help me think."

He got out a bun and took a big bite. "Pah!" he spat. "That needs salt."

He grinned. "I know what to ask for..."

At once, the millstone began to turn. Bright white salt poured out.

The thief put some salt on his bun and munched away happily.

Then he fell asleep, dreaming of riches.

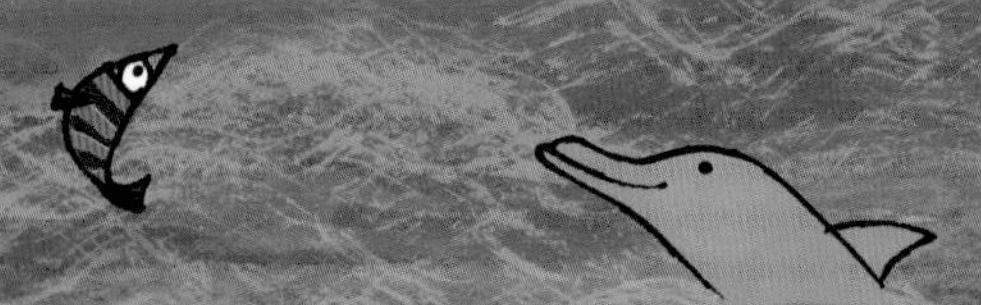

All night long, the
millstone kept turning.

The pile of salt grew bigger...

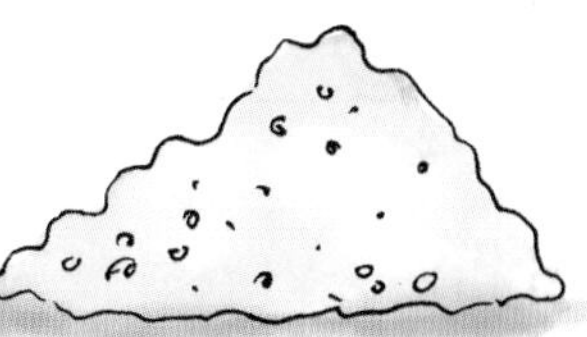

and bigger...

and BIGGER.

The thief was woken by something tickling his feet. "What's that?" he cried.

It was a HUGE heap of salt.

“Stop!” he shouted.

But the millstone kept turning.

"That's enough!" he yelled.
But the millstone kept turning.

The salt was very heavy.
The boat began to sink,
lower and lower.

Soon, waves were slopping over the side – and still the millstone kept turning.

The thief dug through the salt, looking for the millstone. But it was buried too deep.

The millstone kept turning... The boat sank. It took the magic millstone with it, right to the bottom of the ocean.

There it has stayed, pouring out salt to this very day. And that's why the sea is salty.

As for the thief, he had to swim home – where an angry King was waiting for him.

Why the Sea is Salty
is a traditional folktale from Korea.
A similar story is told in Sweden.

Designed by Michelle Lawrence
Series designer: Russell Punter
Series editor: Lesley Sims

First published in 2009 by Usborne Publishing Ltd., Usborne House, 83-85 Saffron Hill, London EC1N 8RT, England. www.usborne.com

Printed in China. UE. First published in America in 2009.

USBORNE FIRST READING
Level Four

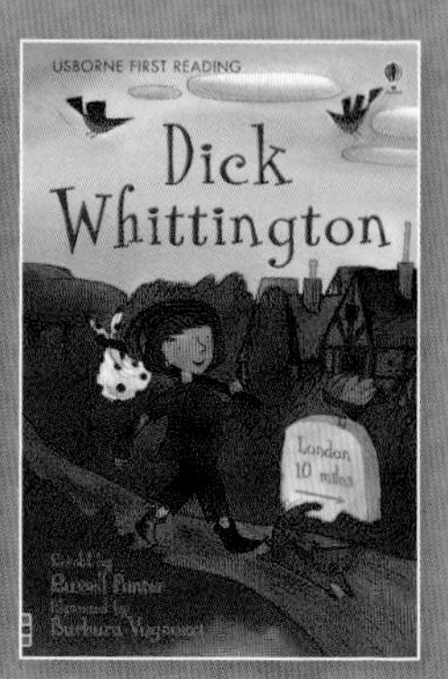

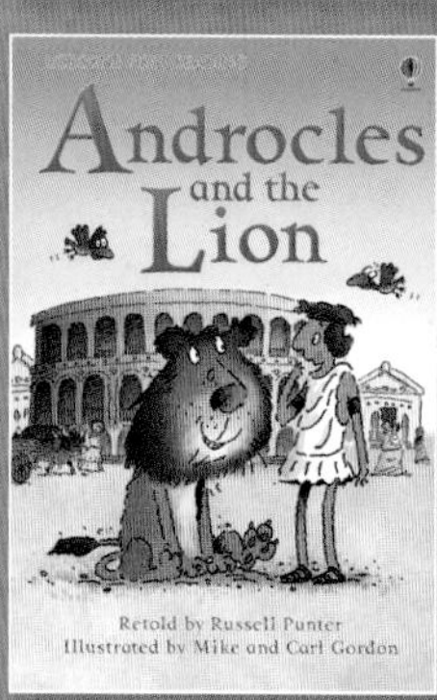

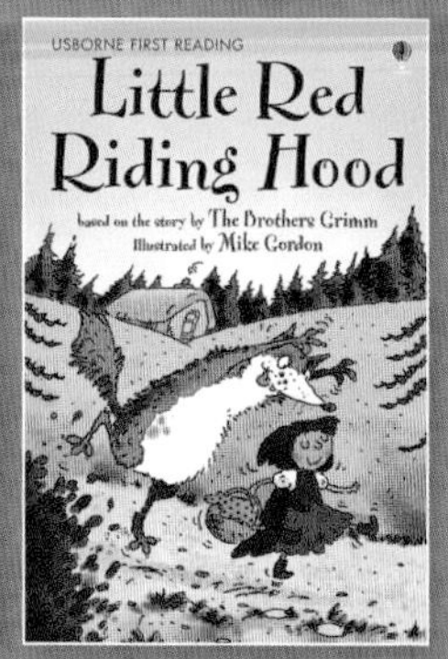